LAND TRUSTS AND NATIONAL PARKS

GLOBAL CITIZENS: ENVIRONMENTALISM

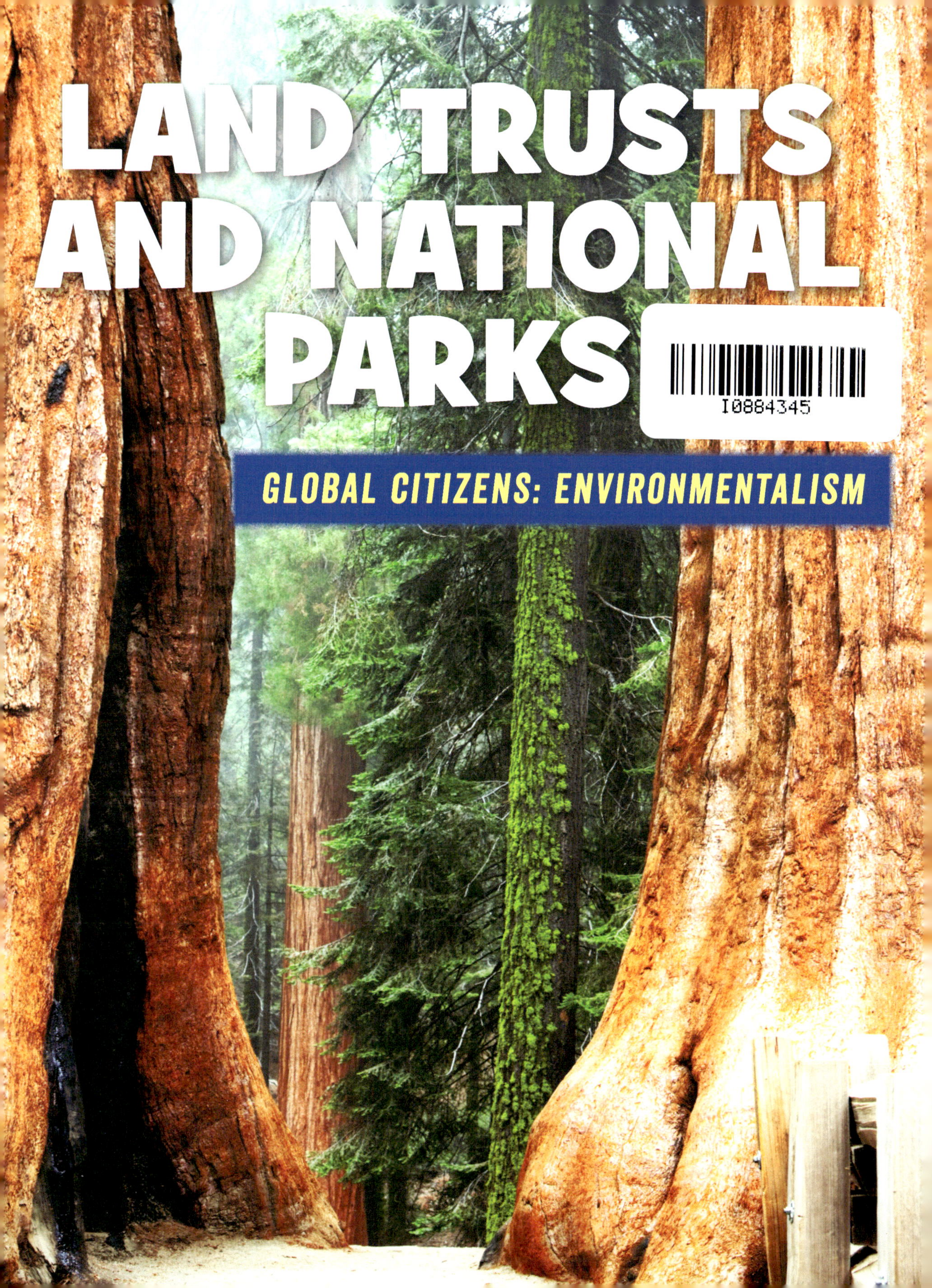

Published in the United States of America by Cherry Lake Publishing
Ann Arbor, Michigan
www.cherrylakepublishing.com

Content Adviser: Michael Rockett MS, Natural resources

Reading Adviser: Marla Conn MS, Ed., Literacy specialist, Read-Ability, Inc.

Photo Credits: © Galyna Andrushko/Shutterstock.com, cover, 1; © Lautz/Shutterstock.com, 5; © tusharkoley/Shutterstock.com, 6; © Alexey Smolyanyy/Shutterstock.com, 8; ©kan_khampanya/Shutterstock.com, 10; © Alice Nerr/Shutterstock.com, 13; © Chris Howey/Shutterstock.com, 14; ©lenisecalleja.photography/Shutterstock.com, 15; © martinusnovedwin/Shutterstock.com, 16; © N Mrtgh/Shutterstock.com, 19; © MAKSYM SUKHENKO/Shutterstock.com, 20; © Kris Wiktor/Shutterstock.com, 22; © cadlikai/Shutterstock.com, 25; © Peerasith Patrick Triratpadoongphol/Shutterstock.com, 26; © Keneva Photography/Shutterstock.com, 28

Library of Congress Cataloging-in-Publication Data has been filed and is available at catalog.loc.gov

Cherry Lake Publishing would like to acknowledge the work of the Partnership for 21st Century Learning. Please visit *www.p21.org* for more information.

Printed in the United States of America
Corporate Graphics

ABOUT THE AUTHOR

Ellen Labrecque has written over 100 books for children. She is passionate about being a friend to the environment and taking care of our planet. She lives in Pennsylvania with her husband, Jeff, and her two young "editors," Sam and Juliet. She loves running, hiking, and reading.

TABLE OF CONTENTS

CHAPTER 1

History: Earth's Land

Environmentalism is a big word. But its meaning is simple. Practicing environmentalism means being a friend of Earth and all its creatures. Environmentalists want to keep our air healthy, our land clean, and our water fresh. They want to take care of our plants and animals by making sure our planet remains a safe place to live. Some environmentalists focus on encouraging people to stop polluting. Others encourage people to **recycle**. One of the most important environmental jobs is to protect and save our land for national parks and wildlife preserves. Organizations that work to preserve these lands are called **land trusts**.

Carrick-a-Rede in Ireland is protected by a land trust.

Arches National Park in Utah was established in 1929.

The Story of National Parks

Open, undeveloped land filled with countless plants, animals, and other creatures can be found all over the world. **Conservationists** work to protect this land. They protect land from being overrun by buildings, roads, railroads, and farms. They prevent people from chopping down forests. Conservationists protect plants and animals living in marshes, grasslands, beaches, ponds, rivers, and oceans. This protection allows the creatures to continue to live safely in their own natural habitats, or homes.

The first national park established was Yellowstone National Park in Wyoming and parts of Montana and Idaho. It was established in 1872. Yellowstone is 3,472 square miles (8,992 square kilometers) of land that includes lakes, canyons, rivers, and mountains. The US government wanted to protect the wildlife living there. They also wanted to protect the **geothermal** activity. Geothermal activity is caused by a volcano underneath Yellowstone Lake. Because of the volcano, scientists say there are more than 300 **geysers** throughout the park!

As time went on, more and more national parks were established in the United States and all over the world. In 1885,

This is the White Dome Geyser in Yellowstone National Park.

Canada protected miles of hot mineral springs in Banff, Alberta. Banff National Park now covers more than 2,500 square miles (6,475 sq km). It has several ice fields and glacial lakes.

The World Gets Organized

During the London Convention in 1933, leaders from many countries, including the United States and Great Britain, signed a document agreeing to protect animals, plants, and lands all over

Developing Questions

Every year, millions of people visit the national parks in the United States. Environmentalists believe that all this visiting can hurt the parks. In what ways do you think it's hurting the parks? How can this problem be solved?

A close-ended question is a question that can be answered with a simple yes or no. An open-ended question is one that needs more thought when answering. The questions above are open-ended questions. They are meant to make you think about national parks rather than just answering yes or no.

Over a million acres of land in Glacier National Park in Montana is protected.

the world. The agreement was the first of its kind. More agreements to protect our natural resources soon followed. In 1962, the International Union for Conservation of Nature (IUCN) organized the First World Conference on National Parks. The conference was held in Seattle, Washington, and 70 nations attended. Two more meetings like this followed, leading to the protection of land across the globe.

Today there are more than 3,500 national parks and other protected areas thanks to these early efforts. These areas include reserves that protect a certain plant or animal. They also protect places that were important to history. Northeast Greenland National Park is the largest national park in the world. It has so much land that only 30 countries are larger than the park!

CHAPTER 2

Geography: National Parks Everywhere

Twelve percent of Earth's land is protected as national parks and reserves. In the United States, there are 58 national parks and 560 national **wildlife refuges**. There is at least one in every US state and territory! As of 2016, the country with the most protected land is Venezuela. Fifty-three percent of its land is protected. This area includes the Andes Mountains and the Amazon rainforest.

Every Park Is Different

National parks are like snowflakes—no two are exactly the same. The world's largest national park is in Greenland. It is mostly covered in ice. Polar bears and walruses make their home there. People visit to see the **northern lights**, a brilliant light

Angel Falls in Canaima National Park in Venezuela is the highest waterfall in the world.

Only certain people have access to Greenland's national park due to its massive size and unique isolation.

Despite its small size, there are many trails and camping grounds in Penang National Park.

show produced by the sun. The smallest national park in the world is Penang National Park on Penang Island in Malaysia. It is only 4.6 square miles (12 sq km), but it is home to more than 417 **species** of plants and 143 species of animals.

Homes of Animals

Many people visit national parks to see both the land and the animals. Kruger National Park in South Africa is home to 147 different types of mammals, including lions, elephants, buffalo, leopards, and rhinoceros. Komodo National Park in Indonesia is

Wild Komodo dragons can be found only in certain parts of Indonesia.

home to the world's largest lizard, the Komodo dragon. It is more than 10 feet (3 meters) long and weighs more than 150 pounds (68 kilograms). That's a heavy lizard!

Gathering and Evaluating Sources

Different types of maps show different things to people. A political map shows the borders of countries and states. Physical maps show landscape features, such as mountains and rivers. Conservationists use maps that help them with their work. The map from National Geographic *shows where the protected areas are around the world. Check out the map at www.nationalgeographic.com/ngm/0610/feature1/map.html.*

CHAPTER 3

Civics: Everybody Helps

Different governments and private organizations around the world do the work of land conservation. Both sides work together to help protect our planet.

International Work

The IUCN is a union of both government and private organizations. This dedicated team has 1,300 members and uses 16,000 experts to help protect nature. Members of the IUCN meet every four years at the World Conservation Congress to talk about the world's most pressing environmental issues. In 2016, this meeting was held in Hawaii and drew leaders from across the

The IUCN protects the Great Victoria Desert in Australia for scientific research. It is a strict nature reserve.

The Land Trust Alliance is committed to connecting people to nature.

world. They worked to establish new international laws protecting more areas of forests and seas.

Land Trust Work

The Land Trust Alliance is an organization that works with more than 1,100 land trusts across the United States. Land trusts are organizations that work to preserve land. One of the alliance's main goals is for every person in the United States to live within 10 minutes of a park, nature trail, or green space.

The Nature Conservancy is a worldwide organization that also works to protect our natural lands. It realizes that the world

Developing Claims and Using Evidence

The world has a lot of problems. People are homeless, wars are being fought, and some people don't have enough food to eat. Does this mean that preserving our land and national parks isn't important? Do some research at your local library and on the Internet. Using the evidence you find, form your own opinion on this subject. What do you think?

The Nature Conservancy helped establish Great Sand Dunes National Park in Colorado.

population is quickly growing. In 1804, more than a billion people lived on Earth. Today, that number is over 7 billion. All these people need more land where they can live, build, and grow food. The Nature Conservancy understands these needs, but it also knows that nature should be protected. Since the organization began in 1951, it has conserved more than 119 million acres (48 million hectares) of land and thousands of miles of rivers all over the world.

CHAPTER 4

Economics: The Cost of National Parks

In October 2014, the US government shut down for 16 days. This meant all the national parks had to shut down, too. People couldn't visit them, so they didn't spend money at the hotels and restaurants near the parks. In those 16 days, it was estimated that businesses around the parks missed out on billions of dollars that people would have spent.

The good news is the parks haven't been shut down since then. In 2015, 305 million people visited the 58 national parks in the United States. This is the most visitors in one year since the national park system was created 100 years ago. All these people spent $16.9 billion in the nearby communities! The money went toward hotels, restaurants, and grocery stores. These visitors

Grand Teton National Park in Wyoming has over 200 miles (320 km) of hiking trails.

Some national parks, like the Grand Canyon, require entrance fees. This helps maintain and improve the parks.

also helped create 295,300 more jobs that year in these same industries.

National parks require billions of dollars a year to keep them running. More than 20,000 people work for the National Park Service in the United States. These people have to be paid.

Top Five Most Visited National Parks in the United States in 2015

1. *Great Smoky Mountains: 10,712,674 visitors*
2. *Grand Canyon: 5,520,736 visitors*
3. *Rocky Mountain: 4,155,916 visitors*
4. *Yosemite: 4,150,217 visitors*
5. *Yellowstone: 4,097,710 visitors*

Great Smoky Mountains National Park was established in 1934.

Taking Informed Action

Do you want to support land conservation and national parks? There are many ways you can get involved and many different organizations that you can explore. Check them out online. Here are three to start your search.

- *National Park Service: Discover ways you can get involved.*
- *Find Your Park: Find the closest national park near you.*
- *National Parks Conservation Association: Learn more about national parks.*

Additionally, parks require money to keep them maintained. Most of this money comes from taxes that we pay to our government. Is all this tax money worth it? Many people think so. Studies have demonstrated that spending time in nature makes us healthier, happier, and smarter. National parks aren't just good for our planet; they are good for us, too.

Communicating Conclusions

Before reading this book, did you know a lot about national parks around the world? Now that you know more, why do you think the work of preserving and taking care of them is an important issue? Share your knowledge about protecting our land and our plants and animals. Every week, look up different organizations that support all forms of land and wildlife conservation. Share what you learn with friends at school or with family at home.

Think About It

There are more than 7 billion people living on Earth. It is estimated that by 2050, 9.7 billion people will live here. Population growth and protecting our natural land are linked together. The more people on our planet, the more people will need space to live and land to grow their food. What does this information reveal about large populations and land conservation? Use data to support your argument.

For More Information

FURTHER READING

Compton, Don, Dave Ember, and Bruce Foster. *America's National Parks: A Pop-Up Book*. Helena, MT: Farcountry Press, 2013.

Zschock, Martha. *Journey Around Our National Parks*. Carlisle, MA: Commonwealth Editions, 2016.

WEB SITES

Every Kid in a Park
www.everykidinapark.gov
Find out how you can visit national parks for free.

National Geographic Kids—National Parks
www.kids.nationalgeographic.com/explore/nature/national-parks
Learn more about national parks.

GLOSSARY

conservationists (kahn-sur-VAY-shuhn-ists) people who work to save and conserve Earth and all the life on it

environmentalism (en-vye-ruhn-MEN-tuhl-iz-uhm) working to protect the air, water, animals, and plants from pollution and other harmful things

geothermal (jee-oh-THUR-muhl) relating to activity from the internal heat of the earth

geysers (GYE-zurz) hot springs that send up fountain-like jets of water and steam into the air

land trusts (LAND TRUHSTS) private organizations that work to conserve land

northern lights (NOR-thuhrn LITES) collisions between electrically charged particles from the sun, causing bright, colorful streaks of light in the night sky in northern parts of the world

recycle (ree-SYE-kuhl) to break something down in order to make something new from it

species (SPEE-sheez) a group of animals that are the same type or breed

wildlife refuges (WILDE-life REF-yooj-iz) places of safety for animals to live

INDEX